Way-out Day Out

Rob Alcraft

OXFORD
UNIVERSITY PRESS

OXFORD
UNIVERSITY PRESS

Great Clarendon Street, Oxford, OX2 6DP, United Kingdom

Oxford University Press is a department of the University of Oxford. It furthers the University's objective of excellence in research, scholarship, and education by publishing worldwide. Oxford is a registered trade mark of Oxford University Press in the UK and in certain other countries

British Library Cataloguing in Publication Data
Data available

978-0-19-830807-2

10 9 8 7 6 5

Paper used in the production of this book is a natural, recyclable product made from wood grown in sustainable forests. The manufacturing process conforms to the environmental regulations of the country of origin.

Printed in China by Golden Cup

Acknowledgements

Series Editor: Nikki Gamble
Illustrations by Philip Giordano

Cover photograph: Denis Tabler/Shutterstock

The publishers would like to thank the following for the permission to reproduce photographs: p5: OUP/Corbis; p10-11: Shutterstock; p15: Shutterstock; p18: Tristan3D/Alamy; p20-21: Vadim Sadovski/Shutterstock; p20: CVADRAT/Shutterstock.

All other images provided by NASA and Oxford University Press

Contents

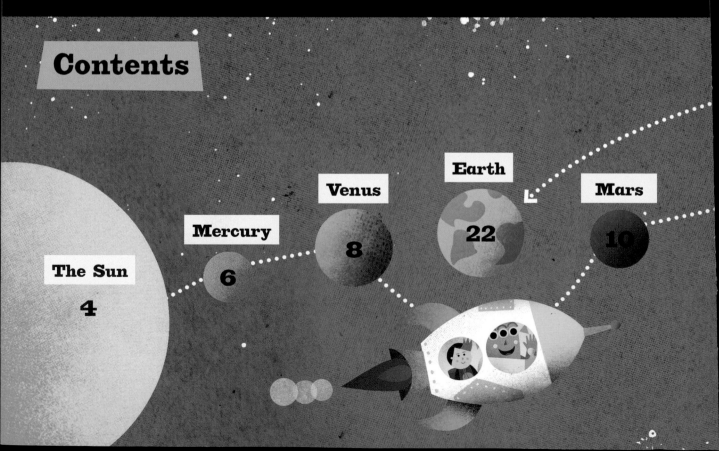

Come on, **earthling**. We're going on an adventure — space is waiting!

The Sun

This is a perfect and **way-out** place to begin. The sun is the middle of your **solar system**. Everything else whizzes around it. It's a super-big, super-bright, burning ball of **gas**.

It's super-hot, too. If you get too close – *puff*! You'll burn up in a flash.

Massive, isn't it?

The sun is a **star**. The stars you see at night are like our sun, but much further away.

the sun	5700°C
pizza oven	200°C

Mercury

On Mercury you'll fry or you'll freeze!
It's really quite extreme.

Days are hotter than an earthling oven. Nights
are four times colder than your North Pole.

There's plenty of time to enjoy a day on
Mercury – every day is 59 Earth-days long!

Mercury is a rocky ball, about the size of Earth's **moon**.

Mercury today		430°C
boiling kettle		100°C
North Pole		− 40°C
Mercury tonight		− 180°C

Venus

This is what you call exciting!

If you went down there, you would get squashed like a tomato because the **atmosphere** is so heavy. Then you would get roasted! The thick clouds of gas trap a lot of heat.

Out you get!

What?!

Only kidding, earthling.

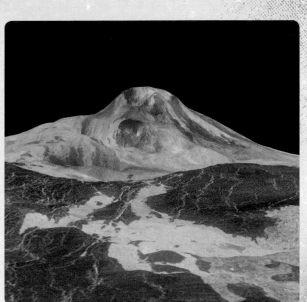

This is the surface of Venus.

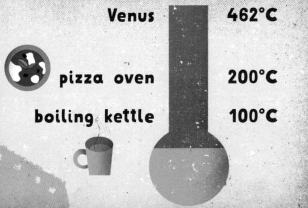

Venus		462°C
pizza oven		200°C
boiling kettle		100°C

Mars

You'll like Mars – it's pretty. It has red rocks, a pink sky, and pink and blue clouds. There's loads to see, like the biggest volcano in your solar system. There's frozen water, dried-out rivers, exciting dust storms...

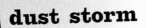

dust storm

Hang on, wasn't that Earth we just passed?

Don't worry, earthling – we're going back later.

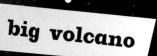

big volcano

Mars is cold and rocky.

melting ice	0°C
Mars today	– 5°C
Mars tonight	– 87°C

Jupiter

Guess what, earthling? This planet has no ground!

Jupiter is mostly gas, not rock. A giant ball of gas! It's all cloudy and gassy on the outside. Inside, the gas gets squashed and that makes it soupy and thick.

It's like a gooey sweet with moons whizzing around it!

Wow! All that is gas?

This is Io (*say* igh-oa), one of Jupiter's 67 moons. It's covered in erupting volcanoes.

melting ice	0°C
North Pole	- 40°C
Jupiter	- 148°C

Jupiter's Great Red Spot is a giant storm.

Saturn

Don't you just love these rings? They're made of lumps of rock and ice circling around. Dreamy, aren't they?

Saturn has more than 60 moons, too.

rings

Is there any ground?

No. Saturn is another giant ball of gas.

This is the moon, Enceladus (*say* en-sel-a-dus). It has a fizzy ocean bubbling away inside it.

melting ice	0°C
North Pole	- 40°C
Saturn	- 178°C

Uranus

If you like summer, earthling, then Uranus is your planet. Summers here are 21 Earth-years long. And it's total daylight, all the time!

The trouble is, Uranus is so far from the sun that it's not exactly warm. This big ball of gas is *freezing*!

Let's spot some more moons.

There's a moon!

And another!

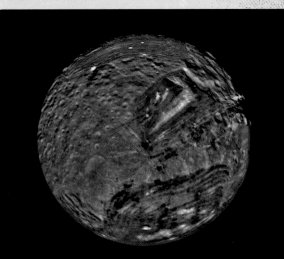

This is Miranda, one of
Uranus's 27 moons.

melting ice		0°C
North Pole		- 40°C
Uranus		- 216°C

Aagghhh!

Neptune

Neptune's another giant gas ball. There's no ground to hit, so how about a skydive?

If you drop into those clouds, you'll hit winds faster than a fighter jet. You'll fall and fall, and then the crush of ice and gas will squash you flat! Ouch!

Fastest winds in the solar system

This is Triton, one of Neptune's 13 moons.

melting ice	0°C
North Pole	- 40°C
Neptune	- 214°C

Pluto and Beyond

Poor little rocky Pluto, way out on the edge of your solar system. You earthlings won't count it as a proper planet. You call it a **dwarf planet**.

Well, I like Pluto. It's so small there's hardly any **gravity** to hold anything on the ground — so it's perfect for giant leaps!

Time to get you home.

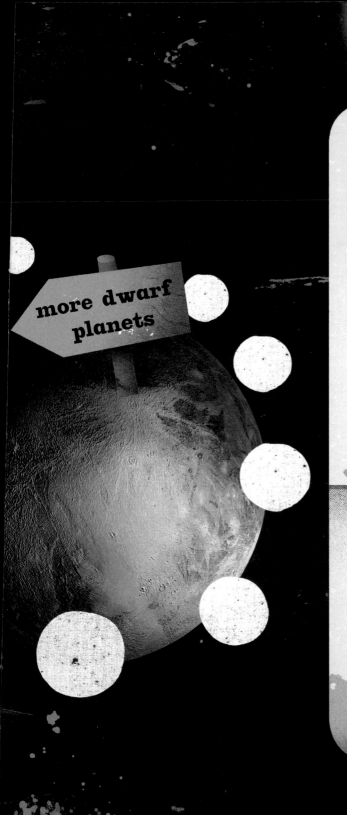

more dwarf planets

Voyager 1

This spacecraft has gone beyond Pluto and left our solar system. It has travelled further than anything else in human history.

melting ice	0°C
North Pole	- 40°C
Pluto	- 233°C

Earth

Call me an alien, but Earth really is way-out.

That comfy atmosphere full of air and cloud keeps it just right for you earthlings. Your heads won't boil and you can breathe.

And all that life! Crawly things, wiggly things – even vegetables! Freaky!

life

That's your planet, earthling.

Earth is awesome!

life

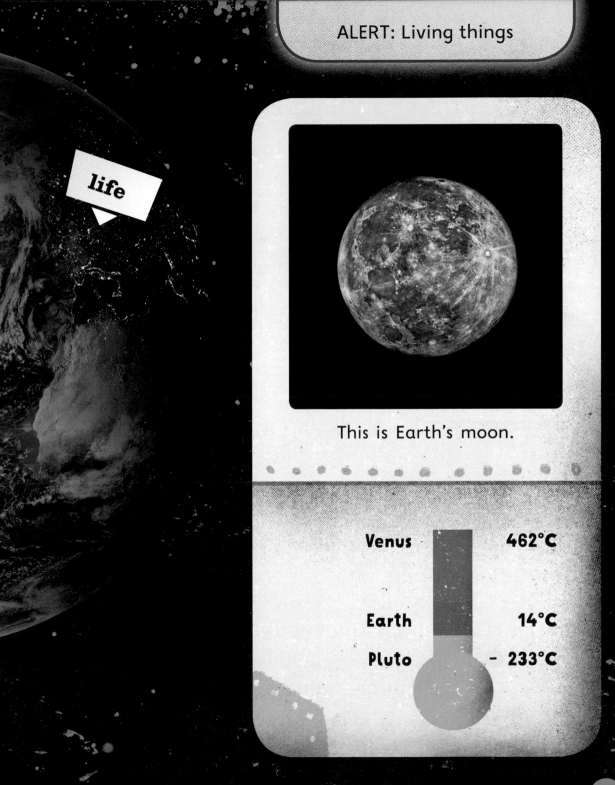

This is Earth's moon.

Venus	462°C
Earth	14°C
Pluto	- 233°C

Glossary

atmosphere: the layer of gas and cloud around a planet

°C: short for degrees Celsius, we use it to measure how hot or cold something is

days: days on Earth last 24 hours. That's how long it takes for the Earth to spin around once.

dwarf planet: a small planet

earthling: someone who lives on Earth

gas: something that isn't solid like rock, or liquid like water.

gravity: it pulls us down towards the ground so we stay on it

moon: a ball of rock or sometimes ice that circles a planet

planet: a big round ball of rock or gas that goes around a star

solar system: the group of planets that circles around a star, such as our sun

star: a big, very bright fiery ball, like our sun, but much, much further away

way-out: very unusual or crazy

Index

Bye!